The Story of
LAO TZU

www.royalcollins.com

Picture Story Book of Ancient Chinese Thinkers

The Story of LAO TZU

Guo Defu

Translated by Wu Meilian

Books Beyond Boundaries

ROYAL COLLINS

Picture Story Books of Ancient Chinese Thinkers
The Story of LAO TZU

Guo Defu
Translated by Wu Meilian

First published in 2024 by Royal Collins Publishing Group Inc.
Groupe Publication Royal Collins Inc.
BKM Royalcollins Publishers Private Limited

Headquarters: 550-555 boul. René-Lévesque O Montréal
(Québec) H2Z1B1 Canada
India office: 805 Hemkunt House, 8th Floor, Rajendra Place,
New Delhi 110 008

ISBN: 978-1-4878-1162-4

To find out more about our publications, please visit www.royalcollins.com.

Follow Lao Tzu's footsteps and discover his extraordinary life.

Lao Tzu, the cowherd who loved observing nature.

As a young student, Lao Tzu safeguarded ancient texts.

He met with Confucius and wrote the *Dao De Jing*.

In his daily life and friendships, he shared his thoughts on the world.

He explored and understood the wonders of nature.

He also taught us to admire and respect everything in the universe.

This book is full of wise words that will inspire and guide you.

Lao Tzu was born in Hu County (today's Luyi County, Henan Province), the State of Chu, around 571 BCE, during the Spring and Autumn Period.

His father, Li Qian, and mother, Yishou, named him Li Er, with the courtesy name Dan.

As a child, Li Er worked as a shepherd boy to support the family. When he herded the cows, he looked at the sky, the water, the trees, and the clouds around him.

He watched how the seasons changed and wondered about nature's secrets.

One day, on his way back home, Li saw a group of children arguing around a big tree.

When they saw him, the children asked Li to help them decide what kind of tree it was.

Li looked at the tree carefully and felt puzzled. It looked like a Chinese scholar tree on the one side but a chinaberry on the other. What on earth was it?

After some careful observation and thought, Li realized that a Chinese scholar tree and a chinaberry tree had grown too close together when they were young and eventually became part of each other after many years.

Li told the other children about his discovery and named the tree *hehuan*, the "combined joy."

Sometime later, Li became the disciple of Shang Rong, a local hermit, who found Li to be an extraordinarily intelligent young thinker and thus became devoted to teaching the boy everything he knew.

After a few years of study with Shang Rong, young Li improved tremendously in his intelligence and understanding of life and nature.

Shang Rong was very pleased by his student's achievement and potential, and he sponsored Li to continue his study with Chang Cong in Luoyi, the capital of the State of Zhou.

Before he left, Li visited Shang Rong and wished to hear his teachings one last time.

"Get off the vehicle when you are passing your hometown. Do you know why?" asked Shang Rong.

"Do you mean to remind me not to forget about my hometown and fellow countrymen?" asked Li Er.

Shang Rong approved. "Walk quickly and carefully when you are passing your elders. Do you understand?"

"Do you mean to remind me to respect old people?" asked Li Er.

Shang Rong approved. He opened his mouth and asked Li what he saw.

"Your teeth (that were hard) are gone, but your tongue (that is soft) is still there."

"Remember, the soft stays longer than the hard. When you see your tongue, think about my lesson for you today of preserving the softness in you."

Li Er took his teacher's words to heart and set off for his journey to Luoyi.

On his way, Li took time to examine every historical site he came across.

At the site of King Taihao's tomb, he was impressed and inspired by the ancient image of the dragon created by the legendary emperor Fuxi. His mind wandered away in the misty wilderness, pondering the dragon culture.

One day, when Li Er was cooking his meal over an open fire, a beggar came asking for food.

"It's not ready yet. Can you please wait?" asked Li.

The beggar, however, turned and left.

Li ran up to him and gave him the food once it was done.

“You are a man of great kindness!” Deeply touched, the beggar gave Li a bundle of scripted bamboo slips in return.

"I received these strips from an old man. It's a shame to burn them as firewood, so you may have it, kind scholar," said the beggar.

Li Er looked and immediately realized the value of the writings on the slips, and he began to study them day and night. Slowly, he was enlightened by the idea of constant change, which was the essence of nature, stimulated by the interactions and inter-transformations between opposite existences.

This understanding helped Li achieve a new breakthrough in his thinking about the nature of things.

After a long journey, Li finally arrived at Luoyi. To his surprise, the person who opened the door at Chang Cong's house was no other than his teacher Shang Rong!

Master and disciple were very happy to see each other, and Li told all his experiences to Shang, who listened with a happy smile.

When Li asked about Chang Cong's whereabouts, Shang laughed and said, "I am Shang Rong. Chang Cong is me."

Li Er realized that his teacher had put him through a test.

Later, Shang Rong introduced Li Er to all the famous people in Luoyi.

Li devoted himself to learning, and he soon became erudite in all subjects and all classics. In 551 BCE, Li was appointed an official in the Zhou State Library.

This provided him with an invaluable opportunity to read all the important books available at the time. He arranged the existing materials and transcribed some precious manuscripts, keeping the library organized and vigorous.

As his work gradually stabilized, Li also became a husband and a father. His son's name was Li Zong. Li often took his son for a walk by the Chan River and taught him about the world around him.

Both Li and his wife loved tree peonies. One day, his wife met a florist who was bragging about his tree peony roots, so she bought one. Li also ran into a florist who was silently selling tree peony roots. Li bought one from him and planted the two roots together. After some time, Li's tree peony bloomed beautifully, but his wife's did not. It turned out it was not a tree peony but a wild bindii, a common weed. "Honest words may not be pleasing to the ears, but pleasant words can be dishonest," thought Li.

Li returned to his hometown and invited his mother to live with him. Yishou was thrilled to see her grandson Zong, but she still grew homesick at times. Li would cheer her up by reminding her of his childhood and acting like a baby when she felt sad.

Li was a good father and teacher to his son. When they were walking by the river, he told Zong that the greatest virtue was like that of the water, which benefited all but did not claim merit. However, when Zong was learning to swim, he also warned him to beware of the danger of drowning when enjoying the pleasure of floating.

Gradually, Li taught Zong the philosophy of living according to the Way of nature. "All under heaven will come [to it who holds fast to the Way] but not be harmed; rest in safety and peace."

Later, Li was promoted to the librarian in charge of writing and recording political events as well as organizing historical materials. As his reputation grew, people respectfully called him Lao Tzu (Master Lao) or Lao Dan. The King of Zhou set up a pillar in the palace hall specially for Lao Tzu so that he could record what happened in court and lean upon it when he got tired. In the following generations, the post of imperial librarian was referred to as the "official by the pillar." After decades of working as a court recorder, Lao Tzu gained profound insight into the state operations, which he eventually wrote in the *Dao De Jing*.

The language of *Dao De Jing* shows features of folk literature with a distinct flavor of life.

This came from the folk songs, ballads, and legends that Lao Tzu collected from different regions when he traveled around with his son after work.

As the imperial house of Zhou grew weaker, the feudal kings began to usurp its power. Lord Jian of Gan was then the leader of his state, but he was unfriendly with his kins, Lord Cheng and Lord Jing, and caused turmoil in the country. Lao Tzu truthfully abided by his duties and recorded Lord Jian's behaviors. Infuriated, the latter dismissed him from office.

Lao Tzu returned to his hometown with his family and became a teacher. A young man called Nanrong Chu from the State of Chu traveled seven days and nights to hear his teachings.

"Why do you come with such a big crowd?" asked Lao Tzu immediately when Nanrong walked in.

The young man, who came alone, was confused. He did not understand that the "crowd" that Lao Tzu said was the many worldly attachments he was holding to, and that Lao Tzu was trying to invoke him to reflect on detaching from those thoughts and returning to his true nature.

The standard dialect of the time was called *yayan*, the refined speech. By teaching students from different places and speaking different dialects, Lao Tzu helped disseminate the *yayan* to a wider public.

In addition, he introduced the writing system of Western Zhou Dynasty in his teaching by using the large seal script written on bamboo slips.

Lao Tzu made an indelible contribution to promoting the use of refined language, bamboo slips, and large seal script in education.

Among Lao Tzu's students, there were many outstanding thinkers who had long-lasting influences on future generations. For example, Yang Zhu, a sui generis philosopher, believed in a spontaneously ruled society where "no one thinks of harming or benefiting others"; Wenzi, the teacher of Fan Li, later fully implemented Lao Tzu's philosophy; Nanguo Ziqi, the teacher of Zhuangzi, eventually epitomized the thought of the Daoist school.

Soon after Lao Tzu returned to his hometown, his mother, Yishou, passed away. Her death prompted Lao Tzu to reflect more deeply on human life.

After a few years, Lao Tzu and his son Li Zong were invited to the State of Lu to observe the Zhou rituals. During this time, a friend of his passed away, and Lao Tzu arranged his funeral, which the young Confucius attended as well.

On their way to the cemetery, an eclipse occurred. Lao Tzu immediately ordered the team to stop and wait for the eclipse to end. Young Confucius asked him for his reason, and Lao Tzu said, "Gentlemen travel during the day; only criminals travel at night. An eclipse is like night, so we must wait for the sky to brighten again."

Li Zong, now a young man, had great ambitions and decided to travel around the states to realize his dreams. Before he left, Lao Tzu taught him everything about state operations and military strategies, and he imparted the thought of "The Way [being] eternally nameless" and that "One who assists the ruler of men with the Way does not use force of arms against all under heaven."

Zong later became a great military general in the State of Wei. He was well-known for applying his father's theory in solving practical problems.

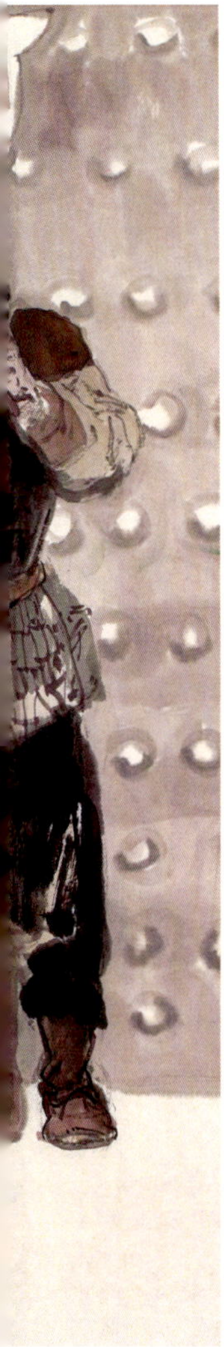

In 530 BCE, Lord Jian of Gan's younger brother, Lord Dao, attempted to destroy the powers of Lords Cheng and Jing but failed. Lao Tzu, who had offended Lord Jian, was now appreciated by Lords Cheng and Jing as Lord Jian's opponent and offered back his old job in Luoyi.

One day, Lao Tzu's student Wenzi came to visit and saw him holding his sleeping grandson Li Zhu. "You see," said Lao Tzu, "this baby can cry the entire day while his voice does not become hoarse. It is because his crying is natural and harmonious. His bones are weak, and his sinews are soft, yet his grip is tight. This is the natural state of an infant, who is true to his nature and follows his spontaneous instincts. I guess this is what we should all strive for."

In 518 BCE, the 34-year-old Confucius, sponsored by the Duke Zhao of Lu, came to study with Lao Tzu. He shot down a wild goose when he was passing the Yellow River, as a gift for his teacher. Lao Tzu welcomed him outside the city gate.

With Lao Tzu, Confucius studied more than 3,000 ancient texts in the state library and transcribed some important manuscripts. This broad consumption of knowledge helped him a lot later in life when he edited *The Book of Documents*.

Lao Tzu invited Confucius to his home and introduced him to his family. "My first teacher in life was a tree," he said, and he told Confucius about the story of the tree of combined joy.

This story stuck in Confucius' mind for a long time, and he realized that the essence and interrelation of things could be explored through their appearances.

During one of their discussions, Confucius expressed his belief in engaging in politics and governing society by virtue. Lao Tzu, on the other hand, illustrated how "Through nonaction, no action is left undone." Society will be ruled by itself if its leader could follow the natural law of things. He then explained the necessary virtues one must have and the detailed procedures to be followed when implementing nonaction.

“Isn’t Shun the sage king an example of nonaction?” asked Lao Tzu.

“Indeed, he is!” said Confucius.

One day, Confucius saw Lao Tzu drying his hair in the sun by the tree peony bushes, calm and silent like a dead tree. Confucius thus asked about the state of emptiness and silence.

Lao Tzu answered, "Attain the utmost emptiness, maintain utter stillness. The myriad creatures arise side by side; thus, I observe their renewal." The best way to understand things thoroughly is to maintain a calm and desireless mind.

Another time, they were talking about a person in Chu, who lost his bow but did not search for it, saying, "A man in Chu lost it, another man in Chu found it, why the need of searching?"

Confucius thought about it and said, “Why don’t we drop the ‘Chu’ and remove any boundaries that separate people from different states?”

Lao Tzu asked, “Why don’t we drop the ‘man’ as well and remove any boundaries that differentiate concepts in our mind?”

Once, Confucius found Lao Tzu collecting dates from the tree for his grandson Zhu, and he went to help.

“This tree was from my hometown. My mother planted it here. When I taste it, I will remember her.”

“I also have a date tree in my garden planted by my mother,” said Confucius. “I bring them to my mother’s grave every year when they are ripe.”

Sometimes, when they went boating in the river, Lao Tzu would tell Confucius about the virtue of water.

“Water nourishes everything but competes with nothing, occupying the places loathed by the masses. It resembles the Way more than anything else.”

Sometimes, they would ride to the heaven and earth worshipping sites to see the ancient kings' legacy and observe the grandest etiquette. When they mounted the Cuiyun Peak, they enjoyed the awesome sight, and Lao Tzu talked about his ideal visualization of human society, in which the state was small, and the people were few.

It was the paradise that Lao Tzu dreamed of. A small world where people lived simple lives, free of wars. Confucius also shared his pursuit of building a benevolent society for the masses.

When they visited a musician named Chang Hong, the three of them talked about the origin of music and discussed the grand musical *Dawu* (a famous musical play).

Confucius spent about a year in Luoyi with Lao Tzu. During this time, he developed new thinking every day and built a deep relationship with his master. When he left, Lao Tzu saw him off at the Yellow River.

"I hear that rich people see their friends off with presents, benevolent people see their friends off with words. I am not a rich person. I shall see you off with words, even though I am ashamed to call myself a benevolent person."

Confucius bid farewell to his teacher. On his way back, he told his own students that Lao Tzu was unfathomable as a dragon.

Finally, chaos broke out among the royal Zhou family, and Prince Chao fled to the State of Chu with official documents and manuscripts. Lao Tzu lost his job again, and he left for Peize, in the State of Song. On his way, he saw rivers and thought about the ocean. “How nebulous, as the ocean! How blurred, as if without boundary.” His mind and spirit were the same.

Nanrong Chu came to visit Lao Tzu in Peize and expressed his confusion about learning. Lao Tzu said, "People approach, and heaven helps those who cultivate their virtues. When you learn, stop where you can no longer learn. When you walk, stop where you can no longer walk. When you argue, stop when you can no longer argue. Stop where you know you can no longer proceed, and that is your limit. Knowing when to stop, one thereby avoids peril."

Nanrong Chu was enlightened. He bid farewell to Lao Tzu after a few days and continued his journey of learning.

In Peize, Lao Tzu spent some happy, secluded time with his little grandson Li Tong. He taught Tong to read and write, and they played with village children, feeding livestock and harvesting fruits and vegetables. When Li Tong grew up, he became a great general of the State of Zhao.

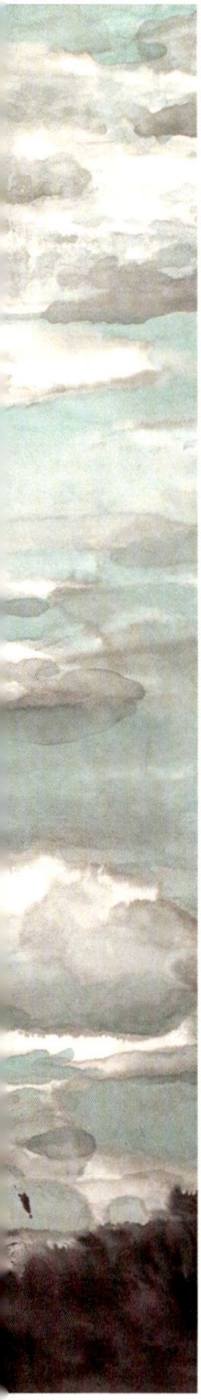

Some years later, war broke out in the State of Song as well. Lao Tzu cried, "When the Way does not prevail under heaven, war-horses breed in the suburbs" (meaning everywhere is a battlefield) and "Where armies have been stationed, briars and brambles will grow," as he saw the deserted land and dying people. Lao Tzu thus left the State of Song and went to the State of Qin.

He rode on the back of a black ox and traveled for a long time. At last, he arrived at the passageway to Qin, the Hangu Pass.

Yin Xi, the officer stationed at the Hangu Pass, was already waiting for him. He was an old friend and colleague of Lao Tzu and had often visited Lao Tzu with questions at the state library. Yin Xi was a good interpreter of celestial phenomena. On this day, he saw purple clouds showing in the east, and he immediately knew a great person was coming.

The two friends were incredibly happy to see each other, and they talked for a long time. Yin Xi suggested that Lao Tzu should write down his thoughts on politics and human lives for later generations, and Lao Tzu accepted this request.

So Lao Tzu stopped at Hangu Pass and began to write. He wrote about everything he had learned and contemplated throughout his life, and it became a groundbreaking masterpiece that would continue to influence all generations to come, the *Dao De Jing*.

"The ways that can be walked are not the eternal Way;

The names that can be named are not the eternal name.

The nameless is the origin of the myriad creatures;

The named is the mother of the myriad creatures…."

In his book, Lao Tzu raised the unprecedented concept of the Way as the core of his thought. The reverence for nature and natural orders became the foundation of his philosophical system.

His theory centering on the Way was the first systematic cosmology in the history of Chinese philosophy, and it cast a long-lasting influence on later thinkers.

Deeply impressed by the wisdom of Lao Tzu's writing, Yin Xi resigned from his post and decided to follow Lao Tzu in his pursuit of the Way.

"What is the essence of the Way?" asked Yin.

"Man patterns himself on earth. Earth patterns itself on heaven. Heaven patterns itself on the Way. The Way patterns itself on nature," answered Lao Tzu. Humans exist together with the world around us, and we can only be at peace if the world around us is at peace.

The ultimate importance underlying the Way is peace. "Rest in safety and peace" is at the center of Daoist culture.

The *Dao De Jing* contains a large number of dialectical viewpoints, such as "Reversal is the movement of the Way" and "Disaster is whereon good fortune depends. Good fortune is that wherein disaster lurks."

The school that later formed after Lao Tzu's thought was called the Daoist school, as *Dao* (the Way) was the essence of its philosophical system. To abide by the Way was the eternal pursuit of Daoists.

Many sentences from the *Dao De Jing* became the guidelines for society as well as individual lives. For example, "The highest good is like water" and "Ruling a big kingdom is like cooking a small fish."

Lao Tzu visited all the famous sites in the State of Qin, and he lived in seclusion in the regions of Fufeng and Zhouzhi (today's Fufeng and Zhouzhi Counties in Shaanxi Province), teaching students and giving lectures. After he passed away, he was buried in Huaili (today's Xianyang City in Shaanxi Province), where he used to teach and was deeply missed by the people.

In Zhouzhi, we can still see the ginkgo tree that Lao Tzu planted with his disciples over two thousand years ago.

The legacy of Lao Tzu is the way of understanding things in our daily lives and maintaining a peaceful mindset both in times of prosperity and adversity. Lao Tzu's philosophy reveals the profound law of the universe and greatly enhances the theoretical speculation of traditional culture.

It shines through history and remains a fundamental theory of thought today, and the book *Dao De Jing* has been translated into many languages and has deeply influenced the establishment of world philosophical systems.

ABOUT THE AUTHOR

Guo Defu is a famous contemporary Chinese ink-wash painter and representative artist of the Confucian school of painting. With nearly 60 years of artistic career, he is renowned for his expertise in painting Chinese historical figures. His work, *The Painting Biography of Confucius*, has been exhibited in art exhibitions or book fairs in France, Belgium, Russia, Germany, Australia, South Korea, the United States, and countries along the Belt and Road Initiative, allowing audiences from around the world to experience the spirit and charm of Confucius and traditional Chinese culture up close.